Expectant

Advent
Meditations

ANNE E. KITCH

CHURCH
PUBLISHING
INCORPORATED

Church Publishing
19 East 34th Street
New York, NY 10016
www.churchpublishing.org

Cover design, interior design, and typesetting by Beth Oberholtzer

Library of Congress Cataloging-in-Publication Data

Names: Kitch, Anne E., author.
Title: Expectant : Advent meditations / Anne E. Kitch.
Description: New York : Church Publishing, 2019.
Identifiers: LCCN 2019000715 (print) | LCCN 2019016435 (ebook)
    | ISBN 9781640651470 (ebook) | ISBN 9781640651463 (pbk.)
Subjects: LCSH: Advent--Meditations.
Classification: LCC BV40 (ebook) | LCC BV40 .K578 2019 (print) |
    DDC 242/.332--dc23
LC record available at https://lccn.loc.gov/2019000715

*For all who have been
my traveling companions
along the way*

Contents

Introduction

*A*dvent is my favorite season of the church year. For me, the primary stance of Advent is one of expectation: it is a season of waiting and paradox. As Christians, we wait not only for the birth of a baby and the coming of the Christ child, but also for the second coming, turning our hearts with hope toward the realization of the reign of Christ. Whether we are looking for the first or second advent of Christ, we are waiting for God to be manifest in our everyday lives.

As I walk through this season, I interrogate my own encounter with the world. What is it like to hold myself expectant, to remain in the tension of looking forward for that which is not yet come and, at the same time, that which has already come? How can I explore this in-between space? What ordinary encounters might bring me through the threshold to an extraordinary encounter with the holy?

Since I was a young adult, I have prayed the daily office, albeit sometimes more faithfully than others. Over time, I have felt more and more drawn to the psalms. In the proscribed readings for morning and evening prayer set in the Book of Common Prayer, all one hundred fifty psalms are read over a period of several weeks and then repeated. After years of praying these familiar poetic passages of Scripture, I continue to discover verses that I have not noticed before speaking to me of God's expansive love.

The Advent meditations in this book come out of my daily prayer practice. I journal, read Scripture, meditate on the psalms, pray, and then write. Usually, a phrase from one of the daily psalms leaps out at me, speaking to some ordinary encounter from the day before, or even that very morning. It is in the dialogue between that psalm verse and the encounter that I discover the holy and hear God speaking.

I offer these now as an entryway for others to move into sacred space while going about ordinary, daily life. In your own Advent spiritual practice, you may want to couple these meditations with reading the Daily Office and the psalms assigned for the day. The assigned readings for the Daily Office can be found beginning on page 934 of the Book of Common Prayer or with the Electronic Common Prayer (eCP) app. Or you may want to focus your prayer on the entirety of the psalm from which a daily verse is quoted. Or you can simply take each meditation as it is presented, an invitation for your own reflection.

The *First*
Week of Advent

The First *Sunday* of Advent

Almighty God, give us grace to cast away the works of darkness, and put on the armor of light, now in the time of this mortal life in which your Son Jesus Christ came to visit us in great humility; that in the last day, when he shall come again in his glorious majesty to judge both the living and the dead, we may rise to the life immortal; through him who lives and reigns with you and the Holy Spirit, one God, now and for ever. Amen.

—Collect for the First Sunday of Advent,
The Book of Common Prayer, p. 211

I pour the remainder of the dry oatmeal into my bowl and consider the empty container. There was a time when this round cardboard carton with its plastic lid would have been precious. I would have saved it for my daughters simply because with some construction paper and glue and imagination the canister could become a drum. A shaker. A castle tower. The body of a train or a dragon or a robot.

Now that time is past, my daughters, young women. I no longer save the empty paper towel rolls or egg cartons or jelly jars for projects, but recycle them in another way. Nevertheless, as I hold the empty cylinder in my hand, I feel the pull of possibility. I stand in a moment of manifold time.

On this winter morning, time shifts around me in other ways as well. In one world, we hurtle toward the end of the year in frantic busyness. In another, it is the new year, the beginning, the advent. I pray to open myself once again to the fullness of joy which is the coming of Christ, child and Savior.

We are each containers of possibility, open to the loving hand of the creator. To be made, remade, unmade, made anew. Now. In this time. In this life. Come, Lord Jesus, come.

Monday of the First Week of Advent

But you, O Lord, are a shield about me;
you are my glory, the one who lifts up my head.
—Psalm 3:3

The darkness gathers quickly as I walk along the path, the late fall afternoon passing from sunshine into dusk within the space of a breath. The lights of the nearby city illumine the path, and at the same time seem to cast a mystic glow, hinting at another landscape enveloping this one. For a moment I stand in the in-between and I glimpse the kingdom.

Lately I feel as if I have been walking in gathering darkness. Distress and dissipation clamor for my attention, and the news of the world and of the neighborhood is simply too much to bear. Too much to do, too much brokenness, too many demands, not enough time or resources or energy. And too easy to forget to hope. But as I stand and raise my head in this moment I am overwhelmed with the reminder that the Reign of God is not only near, but among us. And when I walk this path, any path, I walk within the bounds of God's love.

I seek the purpose that eludes me and somehow I have to be content with this. Knowing that I am called to focus on the now, not the when, and to practice hope. Nothing comes to fullness before its time.

I round the corner for home, knowing it will be full dark before I get there. But I am not afraid. I know the way.

Tuesday of the
First Week of Advent

In the morning, Lord, you hear my voice;
early in the morning I make my appeal and
watch for you.

—Psalm 5:3

I slip my thumbnail under the flap to gently pry open today's door on my Advent calendar. It is a retro design, recalling the calendars of my childhood: a winter scene with forest creatures looking over a snow-covered village and a star shining on one particular spot in the distance. Each door reveals a tiny scene of preparation or anticipation of the celebration to come—all enhanced by a light sprinkling of glitter.

I had to hunt to find the right numbered door this morning, and in doing so remembered this as part of the ritual from my youth. How searching for the day's door carried mystery and delight. How could something so obvious and certain be hidden in plain sight?

In my journey toward Jesus, each day is a door opening to revelation, offering opportunities for the recognition of joy, divine presence, and redemption. Day by day I am reminded that revelations of the holy are hidden in plain sight. Some searching, a bit of attentiveness, a modicum of intention opens the way and the heart to sacred love.

Wednesday of the First Week of Advent

The Lord looks down from heaven upon us all,
to see if there is any who is wise,
if there is one who seeks after God.
—Psalm 14:2

As is often the case with me, it seems to happen in an instant. One moment I am functioning just fine, and the next I can't put two thoughts together. It's time to stop. Breathe. Drink water. Go for a walk.

I honestly think my aging body is my friend in this moment, my lack of stamina a gift. As a younger person, I would have insisted that I should just power through, would have been caught up in the lie that I could power through. Yet even now, I am not immune from the voice that whispers, "inadequate, unreliable, uncaring," while at the same time telling me I can do it all. This is a snare laid by the enemy. I know it well.

Then, with the strength to cut through the cords that entangle me, another voice sings into the moment, one that has been singing all along, "Remember the source of life, turn toward the light, know you are loved."

And I remember to seek God.

Thursday of the
First Week of Advent

You, O Lord, are my lamp;
my God, you make my darkness bright.
—Psalm 18:29

The early darkness still catches me by surprise this time of year. Last evening, I wound my way home along illuminated streets yearning for my warm house and thinking that we haven't even yet arrived at the darkest time of the year, the longest night.

Intentionally, I chose the route that takes me through the historic downtown, where the windows in the buildings along each side of the street display a solitary candle. Something about this simplicity brings me joy each Advent. A reminder that a single flame dispels the darkness.

This morning I enjoy laughter and conversation with colleagues as we talk about sharing hope. This too dispels the darkness. We are lamps to one another, companions along the path, each bearing the light of Christ as we wend our way to the crèche and the salvation of the world.

Friday of the First Week of Advent

My footsteps hold fast to the ways of your law;
in your paths my feet shall not stumble.
—Psalm 17:5

I head out for a walk choosing a path I have not been on for some time. It has been months since I have been this way. I still remember when my family first discovered this trail, not far from our house in the city. We were riding bikes at the time, our daughters in grade school. I had seen the entrance to the path while driving and suggested we check it out. What a discovery, as we rode away from a busy intersection and into the woods. Each time we rounded a curve, we delighted in the unforeseen vista that opened before us.

Now the path is familiar, as I know what to expect around each curve. But it is not the same. The creek that runs beside it has shifted its course, a bridge has been repaired, and the way widened and made smooth. The path has been cared for in my absence. And I bring a different self.

The Advent way too is both familiar and new. The prayers and Scriptures comfort me with their resonance of years past, but at the same time I hear anew the urgent call to make ready myself and the way. Advent requires our vigilance. We are called to be awake to each moment, to anticipate Christ while at the same time remembering we do not know the hour. To keep our feet on the path that leads to righteousness. To repent of our sinful choices, which draw us to walk the way of deceit and fear. To remember that we are expecting nothing less than the breaking in of a new creation, nothing less than Love itself.

Saturday of the
First Week of Advent

For you will give him everlasting felicity
and will make him glad with the joy of your presence.
—Psalm 21:6

I glance out the window and feel a smile begin. It is snowing. I'm not sure when it started, and as I hadn't paid any attention to the weather forecast, I am caught by surprise. And delight.

I know the complications this weather can bring, but nevertheless my overriding response is excitement. To me it announces cheer, it speaks of winter woods and quiet paths, plucky birdsong calling into cold stillness, clean beauty frosting city landscapes.

Simply the anticipation of what these first few flakes may herald calls me into the presence of transcendent joy, the presence of a God who delights, laughs, wants to make our hearts glad. And I am awed that an ordinary water crystal can evoke such reverence.

The flakes become larger, slowing into a steady fall. And I welcome the invitation to revel in the mystery of God's creation.

The *Second*
Week of Advent

The Second *Sunday* of Advent

Merciful God, who sent your messengers the prophets to preach repentance and prepare the way for our salvation: Give us grace to heed their warnings and forsake our sins that we may greet with joy the coming of Jesus Christ our Redeemer; who lives and reigns with you and the Holy Spirit, one God, now and for ever. Amen.

—Collect for the Second Sunday of Advent, The Book of Common Prayer, p. 211

It is when I hear the words of complaint come out of my mouth with venom that I realize I am in trouble. It is not so much that I have noted something amiss and want to speak to it. It is that I am ready to take someone down. I have been collecting faults, gathering ammunition.

This tendency to store up wrongs is a fault line in my soul, a place where the combination of certain behaviors and pressure cause a rift in my relationship with God, and in the worst cases, an eruption of vitriol. I know the warning signs, but I don't always heed them.

Now, I turn my face to my Redeemer, the one who loves me faults and all, and confess. I lay down my complaints one by one. I stop giving them my attention. I stop giving them power.

The sense of a burden being lifted from my spirit is palpable. Contentment rushes in to the space created by the absence of my grumbling. I remember how wonderful it is to place my trust in God. Come, Lord Jesus, come.

Monday of the
Second Week of Advent

All the paths of the Lord are love and faithfulness
to those who keep his covenant and his testimonies.
—Psalm 25:9

Yesterday, the early morning sun disclosed an unbroken sheet of snow covering the back yard. It reminded me of my childhood, when such a sight would have thrilled me with its invitation to create on a blank page. I would spend hours outside in the cold, crafting tracks in the snow, pathways, mazes, games. If I had known then the shape of a labyrinth, surely I would have made such a path.

Now, I see the remnant of the single path I created walking across the yard to retrieve the snow shovel from the shed, the endless possibilities seemingly vanished.

It is tempting on the Advent journey, on any journey with Christ, to think of there being one way, the way, to arrive. Or to believe that a life of faith consists in discovering or uncovering the designated path that God has set before us. But the holy does not abide by such limits. What makes it God's way is to walk in love and faithfulness.

A new day opens before me. The possibilities have not vanished at all.

Tuesday of the
Second Week of Advent

And now, what is my hope?
O Lord, my hope is in you.
—Psalm 39:8

I set the onions to simmer and their pungent aroma begins to fill the kitchen. What is it, I wonder, about the smell of sautéing onions that is so satisfying? Their tang brings to mind warmth and comfort and the gratifying familiarity of the family gathered around the table to enjoy a meal. Taking my time, I add chopped carrots and marjoram and thyme, the mixture on its way to becoming lentil soup for a cold winter night.

I marvel that a simple smell can contain the essence of hope. At times, it is difficult to believe or remember the impact of small gestures. Yet I know the uplifting of being on the receiving end of a gentle word, a moment of listening, a burst of laughter. Small acts of hope can carry us through. They are icons of the One in whose hands our souls are held.

Wednesday of the
Second Week of Advent

Make haste to help me,
O Lord of my salvation.
—Psalm 38:22

I wrap an extra scarf around my neck before I step out into the bitter morning, made colder by the fierce wind that pushes people along the street. Even from within my car I can feel its force.

While I don't like to be cold, I do enjoy winter. I find comfort in wool sweaters and thick blankets and burrowing in with a cup of hot tea. I experience a certain satisfaction in wrapping myself up and feeling protected from the elements.

In the early morning I also wrap myself in prayer, finding comfort in the poetry of the psalms, familiar passages of Scripture, and sinking into the presence of the holy. I offer my thanksgivings to God and also seek help for the complexity of the day ahead, discovering consolation as I place myself in the care of the one who saves.

Thursday of the
Second Week of Advent

Commit your way to the Lord and put your trust
   in him,
and he will bring it to pass.
—Psalm 37:5

"Not connected to power: Your computer must be connected to power to install updates." The popup window pulses in the top right-hand corner of my screen. I am certain several highly paid researchers are behind this bit of technology insuring the message will capture my notice.

I have been avoiding the needed updates for days. Each time the reminder pops up, I put it off for another hour or day. I am always in the middle of something that I do not want to interrupt, and I don't want to commit myself to the time and attention necessary for the task. Yet I know that neither the renewal nor the recharging is optional if I want to stay the course.

If I commit to the Advent way, I commit myself fully to a passage that unfolds before me every moment of every day, a path I must trust is there, a trail that I cannot scout ahead. Grace precedes me as God's route is perpetually updated, renewed, refreshed. Although I foolishly try, I simply cannot negotiate the terrain under my own steam. I must stay connected to the power source and recognize that God makes all come to pass.

Friday of the Second Week of Advent

Blessed be the Lord!
For he has shown me the wonders of his love
   in a besieged city.
—Psalm 31:21

The competent and caring nurse practitioner who treated me. The courteous and capable pharmacy tech who provided my meds. My considerate husband who shoveled our walk before leaving for an early morning meeting. The friendly clerk at the grocery store who smiled as she rang up my purchase. The thoughtful driver of the other car who gave me room to merge.

As I prepare for the day ahead in prayer, I also examine the day before, and consider where and when I experienced God's presence. Looking back, I am reminded of the many kindnesses shown to me. It can be easy for me to overlook these humble acts of respect and humanity. I can neglect to honor the loving hand of God at work in the world around me.

Advent is the beginning of the church year. As with any beginning, it offers the opportunity to seek renewal, recharging, a fresh start, a new commitment to engage the days and work ahead with energy, creativity, enthusiasm, openness, and expectation. Today brightens with the invitation to encounter the holy and to participate in love.

Saturday of the Second Week of Advent

The Lord grants his loving-kindness in the daytime;
in the night season his song is with me,
a prayer to the God of my life.
—Psalm 42:10

It is late, long past dinner time, when we gather around the dinner table for a festive treat. We are welcoming one daughter home from college and celebrating the other's acceptance to the college of her choice. My husband and I also lay our thanksgivings on the table for accomplishments in our work places. And even though we have not come together for a meal, I light the two Advent candles and we reach our hands to one another for prayer, saying grace.

I think of the dinner table as a sacred place in our home. For many years, the two and then the three and then the four of us have gathered here for food and camaraderie. Here we share laughter, we tell each other about our days, and like collected treasure we lay on the table our triumphs, dreams, aspirations. We discuss politics, theology, and the best strategies for fantasy football. And here, we sometimes fail one another, forgetting to listen, or harboring resentment, or just being cranky.

But it is the love that prevails. The ritual of lighted candles and hands held in prayer and partaking of one another draws us together and at the same time transports us into the sacred song being sung all around us.

The *Third* Week of Advent

The Third *Sunday* of Advent

Stir up your power, O Lord, and with great might come among us; and, because we are sorely hindered by our sins, let your bountiful grace and mercy speedily help and deliver us; through Jesus Christ our Lord, to whom, with you and the Holy Spirit, be honor and glory, now and for ever. Amen.
—Collect for the Third Sunday of Advent, The Book of Common Prayer, p. 212

I have already walked out to my husband's car in the cold morning air when I realize I don't have the key. All I want is to grab the bag I left in the back of his car and put it in mine. It was supposed to be a quick errand. I walk back to the house and grab the extra car key and attempt my task again, only this time it is the wrong key. Now I am concerned about time and being ready. Back to the house I go accompanied by disagreeable words spoken barely under my breath. I paw through the drawer where the keys are kept; not finding what I am looking for, I feel the anger take hold and demand my whole self.

An unpleasant mantra begins in my head—I will not be prepared, I will now be late, everything is lost. The enemy's logic. In the midst of the downward spiral, I recognize this for the lie it is. After all, I have been down this road before.

Perhaps a conversation with Jesus would be a better choice. Even as this thought forms, God's bountiful grace and mercy swiftly sweep over me and I feel the holy presence enfold me, and I have to smile at my own foolishness. Why do I always choose the hard way? Come, Lord Jesus, come.

Monday of the
Third Week of Advent

But I am like a green olive tree in the house of God;
I trust in the mercy of God for ever and ever.
—Psalm 52:8

I start the oven at 6:00 a.m., not because I am about to set something for an all-day roast, but because I am preparing my lunches for the week and I didn't get to it last night. In my effort to eat better and pay attention to my health, I am trying to avoid grabbing food on the go.

And I remember that I am under God's care as well, a green olive tree being nurtured. Although today I feel less like a tree and more like a shoot. Even after more than half a century of relationship with God, I see I have so much to learn, so many ways to grow. My spiritual life needs tender attention as well as my body. My formation into the person God has created me to be is not one long slow season of steady development. Rather it is cyclical—planted seed, delicate shoot, robust maturity, decline, and the need to let go—being repeated over and over. Yet, not without change. Each season recalls the one past and reaches forward in hope.

The comfort I find in remembering this enables me to be at ease. To celebrate my vulnerability and embrace this time of renewal. Even as I await with welcome anticipation the tender life of the Christ child.

Tuesday of the
Third Week of Advent

This God is our God for ever and ever;
and shall be our guide for evermore.
—Psalm 48:13

I see the postcard on the floor as I am about to exit the building. A failed delivery notice. I am annoyed because we have been in the office all day. But rather than coming to the main door, whoever brought this notice came to a side door and slipped it through. Clearly this was not brought by our usual mail carrier (who always has a smile and greeting for us).

I am sure the person did not intend to mis-deliver the message. Today, rather than the letter coming to me, I will have to go to the post office and pick it up. What could be a cause of irritation offers the opportunity for reflection. How many times have I failed to communicate, thinking I was clear, but leaving my message at the wrong door? And how many times has someone smoothed the way by coming to me to reestablish a connection? So much can be missed if we are only willing to wait for missives to come to us and not equally willing to go out to meet them.

God is our guide. And what we make of the spiritual journey depends on our participation in it. Sometimes we are called to wait. Sometimes we are called to seek. Always we are called into relationship.

Wednesday of the Third Week of Advent

This is my comfort in my trouble,
that your promise gives me life.
—Psalm 119:50

We are well into the service of lessons and carols when I realize that somewhere along the way I have been transported. The beauty of it all washes over me. On a Tuesday night in late December, people from a wide community have assembled to hear the ancient story. As voices are lifted, and faces illumined by candlelight, there is no doubt we have gathered in the realm of the sacred.

Rituals are important because they usher us into the center of it all. The carols, the decorated trees, the manger scenes. The seasonal celebrations and the pauses for solemn awe. How empty these are if they become routine and we cease to allow ourselves to be touched, transfixed, and transformed.

We do await the Christ child, an astonishing and momentous event. Any birth in and of itself could transport one into wonder. And this is so much more.

The choir voices call out the promise:

This little Babe so few days old
Is come to rifle Satan's fold;

—Robert Southwell

I revel in the words as troubles are banished and replaced with awe.

Thursday of the Third Week of Advent

I know every bird in the sky,
and the creatures of the fields are in my sight.
—Psalm 50:11

I know the creature's presence by the rustling in the bushes. Squirrel? Bird? Chipmunk? I stop my walk, letting the world settle around me. More than my body, I still my thoughts, allowing my senses to expand.

Calm seems to spread out around me, as if I am the stone cast into the pond and ripples of stillness move out from me quieting the world.

The rustling comes again and this time a tentative chirp. Still, I cannot see what must be a bird, perfectly camouflaged even in the bare winter landscape.

What is it like to be cared for by God who sees all creatures, who knows each one, takes note of its comings and goings? And does the sparrow know me by my rustlings? What kind of telltale signs reveal my presence?

I go on my way, nodding a greeting to the one whose hiding place I have not discovered, recognizing nevertheless my traveling companion. Today I too will be a wild creature in the hand of God.

Friday of the
Third Week of Advent

Great things are they that you have done,
   O Lord my God!
how great your wonders and your plans for us!
there is none who can be compared with you.
Oh, that I could make them known and tell them!
but they are more than I can count.
—Psalm 40:5–6

I begin my morning journaling and almost without thinking start a sentence with, "Thank you for . . ." and I stop. For the last several years I have been practicing gratitude. Emphasis on the word "practice," because I by no means have this down. I find it so much easier to list for God the things I want help with, the people I am concerned about, and the troubles of the world that worry me.

I often set myself the task when journaling of writing eleven thanksgivings before I do anything else. I choose eleven because reaching past ten reminds me that there are always more. This undertaking compels me to review the day before, looking for God's presence and for the many blessings that went unnoticed by me.

The counting is just the primer. Sometimes it is as far as I get. But often it ushers me across a threshold into an intimate encounter with Christ. The sacred opens to me and I am awash in boundless love and know that God's wonders are more than I can count in a lifetime.

I pick up my pen and continue my conversation with the holy. I smile as I realize I am almost ready. Ready to receive the wondrous gift that is about to be given again.

Saturday of the
Third Week of Advent

*You trace my journeys and my resting-places
and are acquainted with all my ways.*
—Psalm 139:2

I move my finger along the grooves of the wooden laby-rinth feeling its smoothness. All is quiet around me, my office empty of people and projects. I sink into the con-templative moment, allowing myself to rest.

I have followed so many different ways to arrive at this moment. And any way forward is full of possibility. I know I travel with the promise that God is with me on the journey and in the resting places. God traces my ways: as in finding me? Or as in sketching out my life? Or as in following along as my finger follows this labyrinth's path?

I lean into the holy now, sensing God as companion and guide, shield and rock, hiding place and fierce power. I come to the center, lift my finger for a moment, and then begin the journey outward, heading toward the redemption that awaits.

The *Fourth*
Week of Advent

The Fourth *Sunday* of Advent

Purify our conscience, Almighty God, by your daily visitation, that your Son Jesus Christ, at his coming, may find in us a mansion prepared for himself; who lives and reigns with you, in the unity of the Holy Spirit, one God, now and for ever. Amen.

—Collect for the Fourth Sunday of Advent, The Book of Common Prayer, p. 212

"I can hardly make a little corner in my heart ready for Jesus, much less a mansion," I comment as my daughter lights the fourth candle on our Advent wreath and leads us in the final Advent collect.

"I'm with you on that," my husband responds.

A mansion? How have I not heard or heeded those words before? I have lived with the Advent collects for most of my life and we pray them at our dinner table during this season. But now I am caught up short. I have certainly thought about making room in my heart for Jesus. But clearly my imagination was too small. I hardly envisioned a great expanse of space, beautiful and elegant, clean and carefully tended, exquisitely appointed.

I carry the image with me into the evening somewhat dazed by the revelation. A mansion? But then, what was I thinking? That Jesus would be content dwelling in a nice cozy corner of my heart?

The Savior of the World will need a much bigger space.

And there it is. I hear anew the Word who has been speaking love into my core from the beginning. My heart breaks open, exposing a widening landscape allowing for the possibility of more of God than I had ever imagined.

Monday of the
Fourth Week of Advent

God alone is my rock and my salvation,
my stronghold, so that I shall not be greatly shaken.
—Psalm 62:2

The morning dawns with a pale light that is enhanced as it is reflected against the gently falling snow. But as time passes, the morning darkens. I doubt the sun will shine today.

It is quiet for the moment. No traffic. No plows. The snow ushers in a kind of peaceful wonder. Yet I know this will not remain a gentle storm. Soon the winds will increase and the snow will be replaced by hard icy pellets. I think of those who must venture forth today regardless of the weather, because the safety and well-being of others depends on their presence. I offer up a prayer for their protection, and another of thanksgiving.

As we head into the final days of Advent, I am reminded that even as the journey's destination nears, the way still holds the unexpected. A mild beginning does not indicate a tranquil road ahead. But what remains unchangeable is the promise of God. That we are beloved. That God's way is the way of life. That where there is trouble, there is also strength and salvation.

I lean into this promise this morning, that though I will undoubtedly be shaken along the way, I will not be greatly shaken.

Tuesday of the Fourth Week of Advent

Who holds our souls in life,
and will not allow our feet to slip.
—Psalm 66:8

In the darkness I hear the sound of tires on the wet street as people who have already begun their day commute to work or perhaps make their way home. The weather has changed again, and yesterday's snow has become rain. Even though the dawn will be obscured by the clouds, I know it will arrive just a bit earlier today.

I have come through the longest night. And as if creation knows how difficult the final leg can be, the way begins to brighten as I turn my steps toward Bethlehem and the light that shines in the darkness.

At the same time, part of the earth is fully tilted toward the sun, and somewhere else it has been the shortest night, and rather than waking to cold and dark, people raise their faces to the sun.

Whether in light or darkness, warmth or cold, we now wend our inevitable way toward manger and miracle. Mary and Joseph too are on pilgrimage toward ancient homeland and the unknown, where they will find ambiguous welcome and into that uncertainty love will be born.

And the Creator of the Universe cradles us all, holding us close while setting our feet along the sure way where we cannot fail to find Christ, child and king, who has been waiting for us all along.

Wednesday of the
Fourth Week of Advent

*God takes up the weak out of the dust
and lifts up the poor from the ashes.*
—Psalm 113:6

"Are you ready for Christmas?" Everyone seems to be asking.

"I don't know why people ask that, no one is ready," my husband points out.

And it is true. People have lists of what is not prepared. Presents that are yet to be wrapped. Shopping not finished. Baking still to be done. Seasonal rituals particular to each household that must be in place but are not quite.

And there are those who are unprepared in a whole other way. Whose hearts are weighed down by grief. Whose lives are battered by need. Whose perception of the holy is dulled by despair.

In my own way I have found I have had to let go, and to let go, and to let go again. Of expectations. Of particular plans. Of rehearsed routes. And in the letting go I have discovered both holy space and places in my soul that need the cleansing light of Christ.

The Savior of the World is just that—savior of the world. No one, no place, no time exists beyond the reach of Christ's light and love. Not even the unprepared. And especially, Jesus comes enfleshed in the vulnerability of a newborn to embrace the weak, the poor, and the lost. No one will be left behind.

Thursday of the Fourth Week of Advent

Restore us, O God of hosts;
show the light of your countenance,
*   and we shall be saved.*
—Psalm 80:3

"Mom's going to help me bake," I hear my daughter announce as we enter the house. We have just returned from a performance of the *Messiah*. It is 9:45 p.m. I have no memory of this baking agreement.

"You are the best, Mom," she says as she starts to pull ingredients and utensils out of the cupboards for her recipe that involves, among other steps, making pastry from scratch. And she's decided on a triple batch.

There is no alternative but to dive in. Oh, for the enthusiasm and audacity of adolescents, who think nothing of starting to bake when the rest of us are ready for bed.

I take an advisory role, and then watch with burgeoning awe as she takes it all on. Checking on the recipe, which she has as a photo on her iPhone, she adjusts without a hitch when something needed is not at hand. It is not my kind of preparation. Not at all. I would have set aside a different kind of time and measured out the steps in a distinctly different fashion. But as she dances from mixing to sautéing to rolling out dough, it all comes together. And in the end, I am along for a glorious ride.

Advent is ending, the hour is late, and there is no alternative now but to dive in. Others will have prepared the way, made paths straight, where I have been unable or uninspired. And God watches over all, with her loving and light-filled countenance, bemused perhaps when I forget our agreed upon plans, or think there is only one way ahead, one path to the manger. And I realize that my unpreparedness is its own kind of readiness. Come, Lord Jesus, come.

Friday of the Fourth Week of Advent

Sing to the Lord a new song;
sing to the Lord, all the whole earth.
—Psalm 96:1

As I settle in to write my morning meditation, my beloved silence is shattered by a familiar and well-loved voice. "Med-i-tate! Med-i-tate! We're rooting for you," my oldest daughter cheers me on exuberantly. I cannot help but laugh out loud.

While I treasure the solitude in which I sink into intimate conversation with Jesus, I know better than to relegate the holy to such specificity. On a good day, I am mindful of God's playfulness woven into the impossible swarm of daily activity. If I can pray only in the quiet moments, I'm in big trouble. After all, I am surrounded by the detritus of wrapping paper and unsent greeting cards, the enthusiasm of adolescent expectation, the unceasing traffic of commerce in the city in which I live.

God must be in all these places. The manger might be around any corner along any street.

Perhaps we all need to cheer each other on as we head toward Bethlehem, as we put on a last burst of speed, round the final turn, and run full out toward home.

Christmas Eve

God is our refuge and strength,
a very present help in trouble.
—Psalm 46:1

I finally leave the office store after a complex series of unbelievable but absolutely predictable setbacks. Because of course I am not the only one who waited until today to mail a Christmas package. But rather than feeling overwhelmed, I am buoyed by a sense of ease.

Because somehow or other, we all kept our cool. The man who stepped aside as I was reaching for something on the shelf behind him and apologized if he was in my way. The young woman who patiently explained to me that I had packed my gift into the wrong kind of mailing box. The store manager who waved me into a shorter check-out line, but then missed putting one of the items into my bag and had to perform the transaction all over again. And me. Somehow, I did not let anxiety win out.

I feel we are all being gentle with one another. It is as if we all see and acknowledge the stress we are under, and in the face of it each of us has decided to try a little bit harder to be gracious.

And as I move on into the evening, the grace continues to be manifest. In the man in the parking lot, who smiles and waits until I get into my car before getting out of his. In the driver who slows and nods at me, allowing me to merge. In the cashier at the fast food drive-through who gifts me with an unsought compliment.

It is as if for this evening we each realize how fragile we can all be, and that we need to treat each other tenderly. As if a blanket of grace has fallen over the city like fresh snow, quieting it. As if we have all agreed to be kind to one another. As if we realize our actions actually can make the world a better place.

I am grateful for the gentleness as I prepare to meet the One who is gentleness. Who invites us to bring our heavy burdens and replace them with refreshment. Who is humble in heart and promises rest for our souls. Who is waiting to be born anew into the world and into our hearts. Who is already present.

Christmas Day

Christmas Day

The Lord will indeed grant prosperity,
and our land will yield its increase.
Righteousness shall go before him,
and peace shall be a pathway for his feet.
—Psalm 85:12–13

And suddenly, as if I had not been heading its way for weeks, Christmas is. The Advent path has deposited me here, in this moment. Last night, my heart was broken open by song, by word, by sacrament. This morning, I am still shaken, still vulnerable. How can I invite Jesus in to the mess of my heart right now?

"I've been in worse places," my Savior replies.

And there it is. The astonishing news. The good news of great joy. Here, in my heart, where I can hardly claim I have prepared a mansion, a savior is born. The Savior.

And I am surrounded again by heavenly voices, ordinary voices, voices of the faithful and the uncertain and the distrustful. Voices pure and raspy and bold and hesitant:

O holy child of Bethlehem, descend to us we pray;
Cast out our sin and enter in, be born in us today.

—Philip Brooks (1835–1893)
"O Little Town of Bethlehem"

I yield my unreliable heart and am filled with joy.
Today. Jesus is born. Jesus is come. Jesus is here.

Printed in the USA
CPSIA information can be obtained
at www.ICGtesting.com
JSHW012057140824
68134JS00035B/3487